DEAR ONE

100 DAYS OF ENCOURAGEMENT FOR THE HOPEFUL AND WEARY

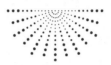

KIMBERLY VANDERHORST

For all those who've been made to feel too small,

too much, or not enough.

A WELCOME FROM THE AUTHOR

Dear Reader,

The one hundred entries that follow are a mixture of poems and platonic love letters to anyone and everyone in need of lifting and support. Some might resonate with you. Some might not. But hopefully there is something here that will matter to you—and show you at least a glimpse of how very much you matter.

I'm not any kind of expert on living a hopeful life. Many of these entries were written with my own personal struggles in mind. And when I first started sharing them, I discovered I was nowhere near as lonely in those struggles as I'd thought.

I hope you find that same awareness in these pages. I hope you come away from this experience feeling encouraged, and a little less alone.

Kimberly Vanderhorst

ONE

*D*ear One,

"Thick skin" is overrated. You are a human, not a dragon. Your skin is beautifully vulnerable. You are allowed to hurt. You are allowed to struggle. You're even allowed to stop for a while, and start again when you're ready.

Be gentle with yourself, okay?

*D*ear One,

You have so many things you want to do, so many dazzling versions of yourself you're struggling to become.

That restless impatience that hums through your bones? That's a byproduct of hope, and of the deep-down knowing that you have it in you to be more than you already are.

And you're already pretty dang fantastic.

THREE

*D*ear One,

Maybe set an alarm or write a reminder for that thing you hope you'll remember?

Tired brains deserve tender mercies like that—and you do too.

ear One,

    you are mountain-wearied
    and hilltop worn
    brought low
    by all your climbings

    rest here with me
    for a time
    let me tell you
    all the truths
    outside your knowing

    let me tell you
    of all the storied heights
    below you
    of all you've already
    become

how the mountain
is beneath you
how it's been under your feet
all along

FIVE

*D*ear One,

Please, don't mistake your soul-deep yearnings for wrongness. You aren't failing. You simply haven't covered all the distance yet between now-you and some-day-you.

SIX

*D*ear One,

You're more than the ripples on the water—you're the stone that made them. Long after the ripples fade, you remain. Solid matter. A deep and meaningful change to the depths of every life you touch.

SEVEN

*D*ear One,

Please don't make yourself small for the comfort of others. You're allowed to take up space in this world—spread, stretch, reach. Embrace the enormity of all you are and all you might choose to become.

ear One,

> you are more
> than this tangle-snarl
> of ache and yearn
> this heart-clash
> brain-smash cataclysm
> of all your deepest maybes
>
> you are stardust forming
> in helter-skelter winds
> as sun-shadows scour
> your brightest corners
>
> you are all the magic
> you have longed for

NINE

*D*ear One,

The people who echo that mean little voice in the back of your mind aren't worthy of your focus. Find the ones who speak the heart-truths you yearn to believe about yourself, and let the others fall away into the silent background where they belong.

TEN

 ear One,

    they might seem small
    eggshell tiptoes across shatter-heavy
    looking glass

    but look how you move
    forward in hurl-bright
    leapings

    look how you move
    upward in wing-beat
    liftings

    look how you move
    inward in hard-fought
    claimings

    look how you move

    look how you become

*D*ear One,

In case no one's told you lately, you are a human person living in a sometimes inhuman world, and the dissonance between the two is damnably uncomfortable and exhausting, and you're not doing something wrong when you feel that in your bones.

TWELVE

*D*ear One,

Would you deny that a newborn baby is worthy of love? Would you ever think to mock or scold them for all the things they can't do?

No. Their worth isn't connected to their ability, not even a little bit at all. They can do so little, and yet they matter so very much.

And so do you.

THIRTEEN

ear One,

the great unknown
isn't a place
it's a person

it's not somewhere
you journey to
it's someone you realize
you've been all along

and once you realize that?
well, that's when you get to decide
who you become

that's when your story
begins for real

FOURTEEN

*D*ear One,

It isn't "attention seeking" to say "X hurts me," "I need help with Y," or something else that identifies your needs. People who negatively label you for daring to ask for support are the concerning ones.

And asking for support should not have to be an act of daring.

FIFTEEN

*D*ear One,

When people treat you like your identity is a "problem," it can shovel your self-esteem so far down you have to build subbasements of worth to even get aboveground.

But people who see, accept, and even celebrate you? Those are your elevators.

You deserve elevators—not shovels.

SIXTEEN

 ear One,

trauma thrives
in the nameless dark
of our unknowing

to name a hurt
is to know it
to map the nuance
of its rending trajectory

to name a hurt
is to find it

to name a hurt
is to bind it

SEVENTEEN

*D*ear One,

We need to redefine what "happy endings" look like. Happy can be found in the "No," the breakup, the goodbye. In walking away from toxic, phobic people and the pain they inflict.

Happiness can look like writing "the end" before the villain gets their redemption arc.

EIGHTEEN

*D*ear One,

You don't need to sacrifice your emotional well-being to play out a role in a cheesy narrative where the bully's right to learn and grow is prioritized over your right to be safe.

You are worthy of your own protection.

NINETEEN

 ear One,

Sometimes
love is words
Sometimes it's silent supernovas
of all the gathered sayings
we love well enough
not to say

TWENTY

*D*ear One,

    Being necessary can feel amazing—until suddenly it doesn't.

Dare to rest if you can.

*D*ear One,

Accomplishment isn't the only pathway to rest. And sometimes, rest is the best pathway to accomplishment.

Rest if you can, dear one. Rest if and when you can.

ear One,

you have called yourself
an empty shell
as if you are food—
a nut, a melon, a seed

but they have not made
a wide enough spoon
to dig out the entirety of you

can't you feel how cities are grass
between the wriggle of your toes?
how oceans puddle at your feet?

TWENTY-THREE

*D*ear One,

Please ignore the pretenders who claim you are a simple puzzle, easily solved. Don't let these sad, diluted people make you feel small. Don't bow to the discomfort of those who view your mysteries as an assault on their pale power.

Their fear of your enormity doesn't need to define you.

TWENTY-FOUR

*D*ear One,

Humans are storytellers, and some stories get so deeply ingrained in the collective consciousness that we feel wrong if we're not following the path of a familiar one.

Our lives don't have to be familiar to be incredible.

TWENTY-FIVE

*D*ear One,

You are not your doings.

You are not the spending and the spent, the scarce seconds and monotonous minutes.

You are not the sum of solitary slices of tremulous time.

You are whole and entire.

You *are*.

TWENTY-SIX

 ear One,

 there is something lovely
 in the way you exist
 all portent and boding

 whirring wheel
 poised to collide
 with slick asphalt
 and fly off, lightning lit
 into the great ever-beyond

 you are a juggernaut
 light made flesh
 pocket-crammed glory
 aching to rise

TWENTY-SEVEN

*D*ear One,

Leaping isn't the only way to demonstrate your faith. Faith is hope in action. Faith can be quietly waiting till someone promises they'll catch you.

TWENTY-EIGHT

*D*ear One,

How you feel is not who you are How you feel is not who you are How you feel is not who you are How you feel is not who you are How you feel is not who you are How you feel is not who you are How you feel is not who you are How you feel is not who you are

*D*ear One,

Each new day has the same number of hours in it.

You are never given less because you used the last batch poorly. There's no arched eyebrow, or soft *tsk* in the background as you're handed your new allotment.

They just come. With a kiss of sunlight on the horizon. With a promise that night will fall yet again, and you'll have another chance to work on becoming who you hope to become.

Tomorrow.

THIRTY

*D*ear One,

You are a cake made of awesome. Being productive, wearing pants, that sort of thing? That's just icing.

YOU ARE ALREADY CAKE.

THIRTY-ONE

*D*ear One,

You deserve compassion for the stupid stuff you do. For the messes you make. For the good advice you don't take. For your reckless, wrecking moments.

It doesn't have to be someone else's fault for you to be worthy of kindness and support.

THIRTY-TWO

*D*ear One,

There's no functional way to live your life constantly prepared for everything. Vigilance is expensive stuff.

Maybe you can let this guilt go? Maybe you can forgive yourself for not seeing every hard thing coming.

Maybe there's one hard thing that can be a little bit softer.

THIRTY-THREE

*D*ear One,

So much of growing up is laying claim to your inner voice and making it truly your own—casting out the voices of those who tried to tell you who you are, or who you should be.

There are few things more freeing than realizing you don't have to listen to them—that you never did.

THIRTY-FOUR

*D*ear One,

Give yourself a little bit of tenderness. Soften the sharp edges of "must" and "should" and "could have by now" with the wonder and joy that is your striving heart.

THIRTY-FIVE

*D*ear One,

Saying "no" is how you shape the world to fit you.

THIRTY-SIX

*D*ear One,

People are tangles—thousands of knotted strands. How ridiculous of us to pick one frayed end and say, "*This* is the whole of who you are."

THIRTY-SEVEN

*D*ear One,

    You are remarkably brave, so please, be tender with yourself. You do not cease to be remarkable when you slow, when the weariness sinks bone deep and collapses you onto the floor of all your high yearnings. Resting is a form of bravery too.

THIRTY-EIGHT

*D*ear One,

   You are an immeasurably meaningful being pretending to be just a person.

THIRTY-NINE

*D*ear One,

    We sometimes use "yes" as a verb—try to yes people into happiness. Even if "no" is what we need. Even if, just maybe, "no" is what they need to hear.

"Yes" isn't a verb. It's a precious, limited resource. And so are you. Be nice to you, okay?

FORTY

*D*ear One,

I say: "I did something wrong. I'm terrible."

You say: "I've also done that wrong thing and feel similarly terrible."

I say: "But you're not terrible. You're just a lovely human person having a terrible time."

You say: "Oh."

I say: "Ohhhhh."

We smile.

FORTY-ONE

*D*ear One,

Life isn't a series of before-and-after photos. Those are just blips. Silent, freeze-frame moments that hardly get their breath before they expire.

You live in the during. You make your home in the long, loud, and gloriously messy spaces in-between.

*D*ear One,

The plate doesn't have to smash just because you don't have it in you to spin it anymore. You can set it down when you need to. Some plates belong on the floor.

$\mathcal{D}$ear One,

Only "everybody" can do "everything."

"Somebody" can only do "some" things.

This is either ridiculous wordplay or super profound. Take it as you need it.

*D*ear One,

You deserve better than you allow yourself. You deserve width and depth and enormity. You are a dazzling sun pretending at being just a speck of sand.

No. You have never, could never, be that small.

FORTY-FIVE

*D*ear One,

    You don't have to leap from Point A to Point B to prove you know Point B is a better place to be.

Too much leaping can = pulled groin. Very painful. Do not recommend. You're allowed to take time to become who you want to be. You're supposed to.

FORTY-SIX

*D*ear One,

    We aren't two halves of the same whole. We aren't puzzle pieces finding a home or lost lines finding a poem. We are entire selves—stars who have fallen into an orbit with innumerable eclipses.

FORTY-SEVEN

*D*ear One,

Never believe the lie that you are only meant to do the things that come easily to you.

FORTY-EIGHT

*D*ear One,

    Not every obstacle can be overcome—and that's okay. Inspirational stories where the hero triumphs in the end are great and all, but they're not the only stories worth telling.

You are always a story worth telling.

FORTY-NINE

*D*ear One,

Functionality is a waveform.

FIFTY

*D*ear One,

You don't have to hate who you were to love who you can become.

FIFTY-ONE

𝒟ear One,

There's an almost ridiculous amount of power in the words, "Do you need to not talk about this right now?"

It's okay not to talk about things.

FIFTY-TWO

*D*ear One,

It's not "lazy" to be tired, stressed, or overwhelmed.

Lazy implies a fullness of ability few—if any—of us possess.

Be gentle with your lovely self, okay?

FIFTY-THREE

 ear One,

    you've fought so hard
    my dear, my darling
    giving all you were
    to become all you are

    you've forgotten what it is
    to lay down your heavy arms
    to lay down your weary head
    and sink into the peace
    of your victories

    rest here
    my dear, my darling
    here where the battle's horizon
    gives way to the slumbered dark

rise here
my dear, my darling
here where daybreak
whispers its secrets to your sun

you are so much more
than the war within you
you are so much more
than a warrior upon the field

FIFTY-FOUR

*D*ear One,

The notion that every ball is supposed to be in the air, every plate spinning like a tornado, is deeply flawed.

No.

Our arms and hearts can only hold so much at once, which means we have to drop things—or gently set them down. There are times when some things very much belong on the floor.

FIFTY-FIVE

*D*ear One,

You are not broken. Never have been—never will be. You're exactly who you're supposed to be. And you can become exactly who you're supposed to become.

If you knew this already but forgot, please don't feel foolish. This kind of truth is featherlight and takes time to sink all the way down into the marrow.

If this is your first time—welcome. Welcome to the idea that you are worthy as you are, worthy as you were, and worthy as you will be.

 ear One,

    you are held
    tucked tight
    against the ribcage
    of the universe
    a tiny pocket
    yearning to burst

    have you felt the
    almost-there
    almost-there of you?
    held back
    till all that you are
    and will be

    Leaps
    Reaches
    Becomes?

deep breath now
we'll catch you

FIFTY-SEVEN

*D*ear One,

You're not broken if you need different things on different days—if what motivates you one day overwhelms you the next.

It's okay. This is normal. And you belong.

FIFTY-EIGHT

*D*ear One,

See that horizon? There's someone amazing waiting there—someone you're going to love getting to know.

Spoiler alert: it's you.

 ear One,

you
are a glorious
mess

a
shiny
tangle

a scatter
of soul
aloft and striving

you
are not meant
to be tidy

tucked
boxed
and bordered

you were made
to be so much bigger
than that

SIXTY

*D*ear One,

It's a good thing to help other people feel happy and loved.

It's a good thing to help yourself feel happy and loved.

It's a *great* thing to learn (and continually remember) that those two good things are not mutually exclusive, and to weave them together into a life that is every kind of joyful.

You deserve to give *and* receive. Please don't believe the lie that you only get to choose one.

SIXTY-ONE

*D*ear One,

In case no one's told you lately, you're allowed to do things that make you happy, *just* because they make you happy. True story. I read the fine print on the blueprints of the universe, and it's actually *encouraged*.

SIXTY-TWO

*D*ear One,

It isn't "lazy" to have difficulty functioning in a dysfunctional world.

SIXTY-THREE

*D*ear One,

Irritability is a natural byproduct of living in a world that wants you to make yourself smaller for its comfort.

SIXTY-FOUR

ear One,

the universe carries you
in its pocket
claustrophobes all that is large
and reaching in you
tricks you into seeing yourself
as nothing more than lint
because nothing feels so small
as realizing you are only
pocket-sized

but don't you see, Dear One?
just how large those pockets are?
deep enough for oceans
wide enough for worlds
big enough to hold all that is in you
that's what it takes to contain you
a vast pocket of star-scraped
    universe
you're certain to outgrow

SIXTY-FIVE

*D*ear One,

It's okay to be a "sometimes" person in a world that's greedy for your "always."

SIXTY-SIX

*D*ear One,

Some people will praise you for your strength, but please don't take this to mean that you lose value when circumstances weaken you.

You don't become less when you're dealing with more. Your worth isn't dependent on your ability to withstand or overcome.

SIXTY-SEVEN

*D*ear One,

      Truth bombs are fun and all, but have you ever tried wrapping yourself up in a truth blanket?

Have you sunk into the simple, heart-healing warmth of realizing you can let the lies fall away behind and beyond you?

ear One,

    they write lies
    across the
    lifeline cracks
    of their hands

    they want you
    to believe
    you fit there
    puny—palm-sized

    but you are
    entire worlds
    pretending to be
    just a person

    so much more
    than they
    could ever
    hope to contain

SIXTY-NINE

*D*ear One,

Laziness has to be a choice, and you don't choose it nearly as often as you think you do.

SEVENTY

*D*ear One,

    That little voice in the back of your mind is wrong—it's not narcissistic to invest in your own happiness.

*D*ear One,

     Quit. Quit if you need to. Quit if you want to. Because sometimes that's the right, wise, clever, kind, and altogether best thing you can do for yourself.

Quit. Give up. Run away.

Sometimes that's the only way to get away from what's hurting you.

SEVENTY-TWO

*D*ear One,

Just in case no one's told you lately or ever . . . it's not a moral failing to be hurt by hurtful things.

 ear One,

you are
a deep kind of glorious

mind-marrow and heart-sinew
sky-canvas and soul-paper

you are
all the most inner workings
all the joy vessels brimming

you are
all

SEVENTY-FOUR

*D*ear One,

That person isn't thinking about that thing you said that one time. Thought you might want to know.

SEVENTY-FIVE

*D*ear One,

    You deserve to live in a world where crying when you're wounded isn't an act of bravery.

SEVENTY-SIX

 ear One,

    wishes are more
      than fractures
     of dandelion
    seed pods

      more than
      candle-brights
      gone dark

    wishes give us
      permission
       to want
       to reach
    to strive

    wishes are how
    we become

 ear One,

Psst . . .

Resting is a form of productivity.

Pass it on.

SEVENTY-EIGHT

*D*ear One,

A good thing coming out of a bad thing does not make the bad thing good.

ear One,

oh my dear
my valiant heart
you were never meant
to break so loudly

to shatter-scatter your strivings
in soul-born shouts
to give your ever-all and always
to be the brightest
best and bettering

No

sink here now
into the heart's soil
where all is quiet-soft
and Rest.

EIGHTY

*D*ear One,

 You don't owe anyone your pain. Vulnerability is optional, and making it an imperative is toxic as hell.

EIGHTY-ONE

*D*ear One,

It's okay to not.

EIGHTY-TWO

ear One,

    you shelter there
in your splintered moment
grasping at straw-house straws
as the wolf blow-blow-blows
you away

away into a
fractured cascade
of helter-skelter atoms
split by this temporary
unmaking

oh my darling
if you could only see
the gathering, the making of you
the way your reckless scatter
allows you to become

EIGHTY-THREE

*D*ear One,

Too often we recycle our weariness into busy-ness, and that is such a hard energy to carry.

There is nothing gentle in the notion that we must always be doing in order to be becoming.

Seek out a gentler path for yourself. You are ever so worthy of your own affection.

EIGHTY-FOUR

*D*ear One,

Being mad at yourself for the trauma someone else inflicted on you is like getting stabbed with a sword and then being mad at your body for having a hole in it.

EIGHTY-FIVE

*D*ear One,

Shame over your humanity is as optional as it is toxic. You don't need to visit the depths of bitterness and despair to find the hope and the desire to soar. You can climb from where you are right now, leaving your shame-anchor in the dirt where it has always belonged.

EIGHTY-SIX

*D*ear One,

Gentleness is a better love story than shame. Write yourself a better story.

EIGHTY-SEVEN

*D*ear One,

You're not failing if you're down after someone knocks you there. That's not failure—that's physics.

EIGHTY-EIGHT

ear One,

    it's no small thing
to find the lost edges
the cliff-dive peaks
between the safe
and the fall

with all the nows
through all the somewheres
catch the whisper-feather
of Hope's plummeting tail
and ride her into the downing down

to kiss the updraft
and soar

EIGHTY-NINE

*D*ear One,

    We sometimes lash out when people fail to meet unspoken needs, hopes, and expectations.

Self-advocacy isn't selfishness. It is so much the opposite of that. It's teaching the people who love you how to love you better.

It's setting them up to succeed.

*D*ear One,

Resting is productive. It's a thing we can produce for ourselves and make space for others to make too.

Productive work. Productive rest. Productive play. They can all feed the human need for forward momentum. They can all help us become who we want to become.

NINETY-ONE

 ear One,

you pushed
till all that you were
and all that you are
fell
into your hoard
of ache and yearn

but you were not formed
of wishes and starlight
you are being made flesh
formed by love and purpose

your wishes to be more
than all your current knowings
have already been granted

NINETY-TWO

*D*ear One,

You don't owe the world your hastily mustered calm in the face of its noise and its whirlwinds.

You're allowed to be a mess when life is messing with you.

NINETY-THREE

$\mathcal{D}$ear One,

Your worth is not tied to your ability.

You know this truth. It roosts in your marrow and clings to your rib bones. It is built into the bedrock of who you are.

But the lies are loud some days. May this and other truths offer you shelter.

ear One,

there is something lovely
tucked into Today's pocket
a secret tuft of joy
masquerading
as pocket lint

*D*ear One,

Resting on your laurels isn't always a bad thing. At times, it can be a necessary thing—to make time and space to see how there is all manner of loveliness in this world that only exists because we exist.

Rest, Dear One. When you can. You are owed such tender mercies.

NINETY-SIX

ear One,

we met just now
in the shadowed echo
of Tomorrow's dreamings
where the sky curls
into the slumberdark horizon

anything could happen there
anything could happen here
we are a pair of lovely happenings
just waiting to be had

 ear One,

you are not just the things you do
things are not the making of you

NINETY-EIGHT

*D*ear One,

    you cannot be undone
    so easily as this

    you fear
    your very atoms
    might split
    one by one by one
    till all you have known
    and been
    gives way to dark

    but you cannot be undone
    so easily as this
    not a little bit
    not even at all

    you are a lovely making
    knit, woven, bound
    by tenderest touch

you will not be undone
so easily as this

NINETY-NINE

*D*ear One,

Recognizing and naming the things that hurt and limit you isn't "making excuses"—it's making room for the very real possibility that you have been shamed for things that were not your fault.

ONE HUNDRED

$\mathcal{D}$ear One,

Just like stories, our lives need pacing. Not every scene can be action. Not every scene can be "save the world *now*." It's okay to rest.

Good night, my dear ones. Be nice to you.

ACKNOWLEDGMENTS

To name all my dear ones would take another book entirely, and the thought of leaving someone out is harrowing to say the least.

First and greatest thanks are owed to Erin Olds, who I'd been toying with the idea of reaching out to about this project. But before I could summon the nerve, she came to me and said, "Kim, I'm juuuuust saying, you probably have enough of these beautiful words right now to make yourself a daily motivation book."

Then, checking first to be sure that my enthusiasm matched hers, she took my scattered scribbles and made them into something whole, and I will never be done being grateful to her for it.

Along with Rebecca Blevins and Sachiko—a friend trio like no other—Erin taught me so much about what genuine support looks like. How "no" can be a kindness, how boundaries can lift and shape us for the better, and how listening to ourselves is a crucial step in the journey of becoming who we most want to be.

I'm grateful to every dear one who has made space for me, grieved with me, been patient with my flaws, and even taught me the gift that those flaws can be. And also to all those who kept commenting variations of "When are you publishing a book of these?" whenever I shared snippets of what eventually became this book on social media.

This is one thing love can do. It can help writers like me dare to keep writing. It can help people like me and you dare to rest if we can. It can cancel out the lies we write on ourselves and make room for important truths.

May your life be filled with dear ones such as mine—with dear ones such as you.

ABOUT THE AUTHOR

Kimberly Vanderhorst grew up sandwiched between the mountains and the sea of British Columbia, Canada. She now lives in the interior of the province where—between the weather and the wildlife—it often feels like the outdoors is trying to kill her.

Thankfully she has plenty of distractions in the form of four fierce and lovely daughters, a delightfully silly husband, and more stories in her head than can possibly be told in a single lifetime.

As a late diagnosed autistic woman, she's passionate about writing stories that feature neurodivergent characters, and sharing messages that remind or reveal just how incredible human beings in general have it in them to be.

She has had some of her advocacy work published in Salt and Sage Books's *How to Write Autistic Characters: An Incomplete Guide*, and *Writing Fat Positivity: An Incomplete Guide*.

You can check out her sporadically updated website: kimvanderhorst.com.

twitter.com/Kymburleev

instagram.com/kymburleevan

Made in the USA
Las Vegas, NV
29 October 2021

33320298R00069